Fabric

by Emily Sohn and Lisa Klobuchar

NORWOOD HOUSE PRESS
Chicago, Illinois

Norwood House Press
Chicago, Illinois

For information regarding Norwood House Press, please visit our website at
www.norwoodhousepress.com or call 866-565-2900.

Contributor: Edward Rock, Project Content Consultant

Editor: Lauren Dupuis-Perez

Designer: Sara Radka

Fact Checker: Sam Rhodes

Photo Credits in this revised edition include: Getty Images: EyeEm, 4, iStockphoto, 10 (left),
11, 15, 17, 21; Pixabay: Byunilho, background (paper texture), GDJ, background (tech pattern);
Shutterstock: Ragne Kabanova, cover, 1; Wikimedia: Library of Congress, 12

Library of Congress Cataloging-in-Publication Data

Names: Sohn, Emily, author. | Klobuchar, Lisa, author. | Sohn, Emily. iScience.
Title: Fabric / by Emily Sohn and Lisa Klobuchar.
Description: [2019 edition]. | Chicago, Illinois : Norwood House Press, [2019] |
    Series: iScience | Audience: K to grade 3. | Includes bibliographical references and index.
Identifiers: LCCN 2018057545 | ISBN 9781684509713 (hardcover) |
    ISBN 9781684043590 (pbk.) | ISBN 9781684043705 (ebook)
Subjects: LCSH: Textile fabrics—Juvenile literature. | Clothing and dress—Juvenile literature.
Classification: LCC TS1446 .S64 2019 | DDC 677—dc23 LC record
    available at https://lccn.loc.gov/2018057545

Hardcover ISBN: 978-1-68450-971-3
Paperback ISBN: 978-1-68404-359-0

Contents

Note to Caregivers:
In this updated and revised iScience series, each book poses many questions to the reader. Some are open ended and ask what the reader thinks. Discuss these questions with your child and guide him or her in thinking through the possible answers and outcomes. There are also questions posed which have a specific answer. Encourage your child to read through the text to determine the correct answer. Most importantly, throughout the book, encourage answers using critical thinking skills and imagination. In the back of the book you will find answers to these questions, along with additional resources to help support you as you share the book with your child.

Words that are **bolded** are defined in the glossary in the back of the book.

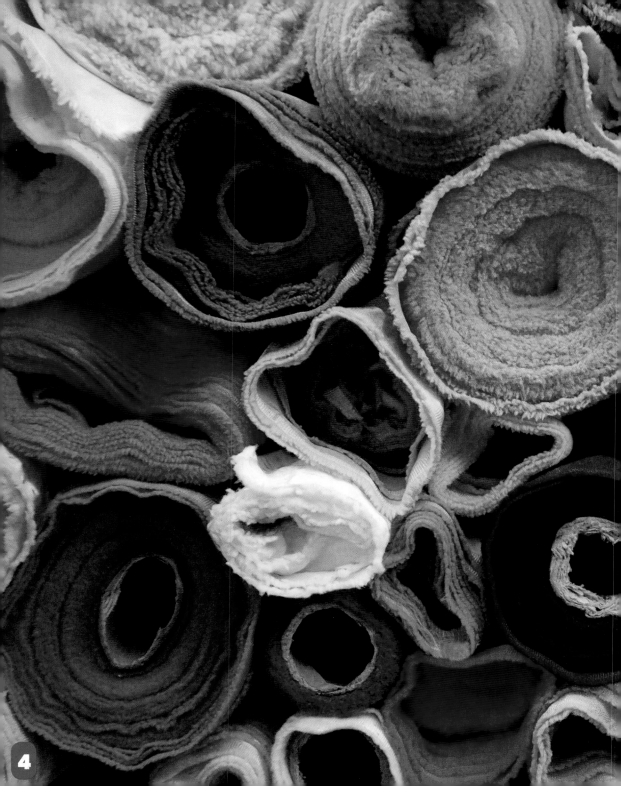

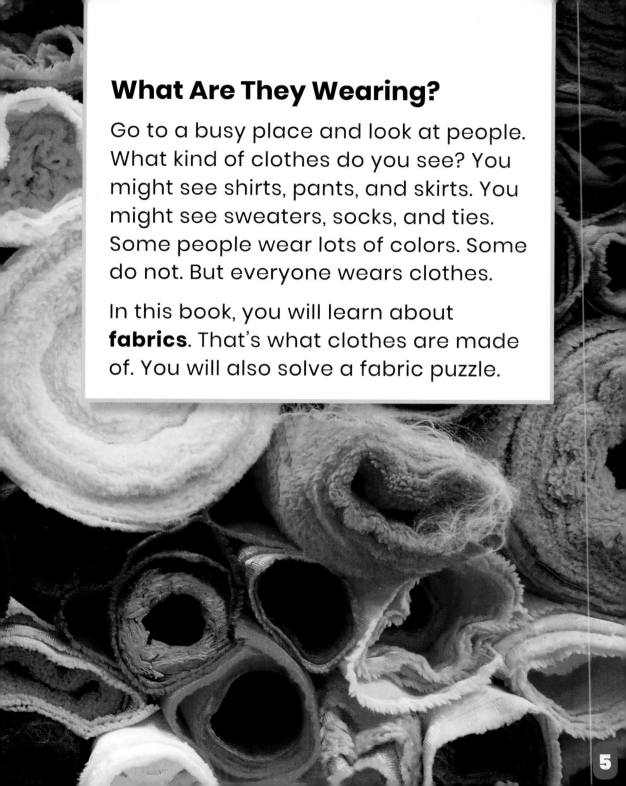

What Are They Wearing?

Go to a busy place and look at people. What kind of clothes do you see? You might see shirts, pants, and skirts. You might see sweaters, socks, and ties. Some people wear lots of colors. Some do not. But everyone wears clothes.

In this book, you will learn about **fabrics**. That's what clothes are made of. You will also solve a fabric puzzle.

What to Wear?

You are going camping with your friends. You will carry all of your clothes in a backpack. It might be hot or cold. It might be sunny or rainy. It might even snow!

Clothes are made of fabric.

There are many kinds of fabric.

What kind of clothes should you pack for the trip?

Here are four ideas for what your clothes should be made of:

◆ Fabric 1:
Cotton

◆ Fabric 2:
Wool

◆ Fabric 3:
Silk

◆ Fabric 4:
Polyester

Which fabric will keep you most comfortable when it gets hot, cold, or wet outside?

Discover Activity

Materials

- cotton
- wool
- silk
- polyester
- spoon
- water

Which Fabric Lets in Water?

Most jeans are made of cotton. Sweaters might be wool. Scarves may be silk. You might find a polyester jacket. Read labels on the clothes. Labels can tell you a lot.

Get an adult to help you.

Gather a few examples of fabric, such as old clothing or rags.

Put them flat on a desk or a table.

Pour a little water on the cotton fabric with a spoon.

Did the water soak in? Or did it drip off?

◆ You can learn a lot about your clothes from their labels.

7

◆ Silk fabric is often thin and light.

Now pour some water on the other fabrics.

(Remember—just ask an adult first!)

Which ones soak up the water and get really wet?

Do drops form on any of the fabrics? Do any of the fabrics stay dry?

How Is Fabric Made?

It's not easy to make fabric. The first step is to find **fibers**. These are tiny threads.

Some fibers come from nature. Wool is made from the hair of sheep. People shave the wool off the animals. Silk is made by caterpillars!

Can you think of other animal hair that can become fabric?

◆ Farmers use special cutters, called shears, to get the hair off sheep.

Some fibers come from plants. Cotton plants have fibers. The fibers surround the plant's seeds. **Flax** plants have fibers. The fibers come from the plant's stems. People have to pull fibers off plants and sort them. The fabric made from flax fibers is called linen.

Some fibers, such as the ones in your windbreaker, are made by people. These are called **synthetic** fibers. They don't come from animals or plants.

Are most of your clothes made from animal, plant, or synthetic fibers?

◆ Raw cotton grows on plants.

◆ Flax plants have purple flowers.

◆ A **yarn** spinning machine creates completed spools of yarn.

Dizzy with Fibers

Machines twist fibers together. This process is called spinning. Spinning makes fibers long and strong. The result is called yarn.

You arrive at the campground. It is still warm out. Do you want to wear clothes made out of thick yarn or thin yarn?

The Cotton Gin

Eli Whitney worked for a cotton grower in the 1700s. Many people in the southern United States grew cotton. The cotton plant has many seeds. It took workers hours to remove the seeds. To fix this problem, Eli Whitney invented a machine called a cotton gin. The machine pulled the cotton through a screen. The screen removed the seeds quickly. Eli's invention could remove the seeds from 50 pounds (23 kilograms) of cotton in one day.

◆ Eli Whitney

The Final Product

The next step is to **weave** yarn into fabric. Strings of yarn cross over and under each other. The strings that go one way are called the warp. The strings that go the other way are called the weft.

Knitting is another way to turn yarn into fabric. Little knots hold the yarn together. Knit fabrics have tiny holes. The holes let air and water through.

◆ Can you see the warp and weft in this fabric?

◆ Knitting is done in many patterns. How many patterns can you find in this sweater?

What Are Some Kinds of Fabric?

Night falls on the campsite. It is getting cold. Which fabric is best now?

Wool keeps sheep warm. How does it do that? It holds warm air in. It keeps cool air out.

◆ Some socks are made of wool.

◆ Most T-shirts are made of cotton.

Cotton fabrics can be thin or thick. But all cotton fibers let air through.

Synthetic fibers are made to be like natural fibers. They can help keep you either warm or cool.

Should you wear the same fabrics during the hot day and the cold night? Which might be better at each time of day?

Silk is very soft. It is warm. It is also very thin and light. That makes it easy to carry in a backpack.

When might silk be better than wool? When would wool be better?

◆ Silkworms spin their silk into cocoons.

◆ Snowy mittens get very wet. Time to get a dry pair!

Getting Wet, Staying Dry

It is morning at the campsite. It is starting to rain. What should you wear now?

Wool can get a little wet and still be pretty warm. Water beads up on top of the fabric. But if it rains hard or snows, wool gets very wet. Then it takes a long time to dry.

Cotton fibers soak up water. Water goes through cotton, too. That makes cotton very cold to wear in the rain.

Silk can get soaked in the rain. But it also absorbs sweat. It can keep hikers cool in warm weather. It also keeps people warm in cool weather. But it's not so good in the pouring rain.

Many companies add chemicals to fabrics. Some clothing has chemicals that keep water from soaking in.

What should your camping group wear if it rains a little? What if it rains a lot? Would your answer change if it were hot and raining? What about cold and raining?

◆ What would *you* wear if you were camping in the rain?

Fabric Designer

Designers make fabrics for many uses. Some fabrics are stronger than others. Some can dry very fast. Other fabrics hold onto moisture.

Designers use computers to create different patterns. They put pictures and colors on some fabrics. Some fabrics are **waterproof**.

What kind of fabric would a designer use for a tent?

◆ Tent fabric needs to be light, strong, and waterproof.

What to Wear?

What did you pack in your backpack? Here are reasons each fabric might be a good choice. These are called pros. There are also reasons each fabric might not be a perfect choice. These are called cons.

Fabric 1: **Cotton**

Pros: Cotton keeps you cool when it's sunny and warm.

Cons: It gets very wet and cold in the rain. It also gets wet when you sweat.

◆ cotton

Fabric 2: **Wool**

Pros: Wool is very warm. It is okay to wear wool in a light rain.

Cons: Wool gets soaked in heavy rain. It can be thick and bulky to carry.

◆ wool

Fabric 3: **Silk**

Pros: Silk is light and easy to carry. It keeps you warm when it's cold out. It keeps you cool when it's hot out.
Cons: Silk gets soaked in the rain. It is hard to clean.

◆ silk

Fabric 4: **Polyester**

Pros: Many types of this synthetic fabric keep you dry in the pouring rain.
Cons: Polyester might not let much air through. You could get too hot.

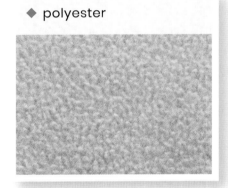
◆ polyester

Can you think of yet another option for staying comfortable during your camping trip? You might want to see what the weather **forecast** is. That way, you will be prepared for the weather!

Beyond the Puzzle

Fabric can keep you warm, cool, and dry. What else can fabric do?

Try this. Put on cotton clothes. Run around until you get hot. Write down how you feel. Are your clothes wet with sweat? How long does it take for you to cool off? How long does it take for your clothes to dry?

Try the same thing in different fabrics. Wait a little while to cool down. Which fabrics worked best for running? Do you think other fabrics would be best for other sports? As you've learned, knowing about different types of fabrics can keep you comfortable no matter what you are doing.

Glossary

cocoons: cases made by silkworms and other insects.

cotton: a plant with a white fiber around the seed that is used for fabric and sewing.

fabrics: cloth.

fibers: tiny threads.

flax: a plant used to make a fabric called linen.

forecast: a statement that something pertaining to weather will happen in the future, such as rain.

knitting: making fabric or a garment from yarn or thread by using long needles or a special machine.

polyester: a synthetic fabric.

silk: fabric made from the material spun by silkworms.

synthetic: made by humans, not in nature.

waterproof: made to prevent water from passing through.

weave: to pass yarn strings under and over each other to make fabric.

wool: sheep hair; also the fabric and yarn made from the hair of animals including sheep, alpaca, rabbits, and goats.

yarn: fibers twisted together; used in knitting or weaving.

Further Reading

Butterworth, Christine. 2015. *Where Did My Clothes Come From?* Exploring the Everyday. Somerville, Mass.: Candlewick Press.

Cotton Counts. 2018. "The Story of Cotton." https://www.cotton.org/pubs/cottoncounts/story.

Hayes, Amy. 2016. *Turning Cotton into Clothes*. New York: Cavendish Square Publishing.

Rice, Dona. 2018. *Weather Wear*. Huntington Beach, Calif.: Teacher Created Materials.

Additional Notes

The page references below provide answers to questions asked throughout the book. Questions whose answers will vary are not addressed.

Page 13: Caption question: There are two patterns.

Page 14: No. Cotton would be better for the day. Wool would be better for night.

Page 15: Silk would be good in situations that are warm and dry. Wool would be better in the cold and wet.

Page 17: Wool might be better if it rains a little. Polyester might be better if it rains a lot. Polyester might be best if it is hot and rainy. Wool would be the choice for a cold, rainy day.

Page 18: A designer would use polyester to create a tent that is waterproof.

Page 20: Another option is to wear many layers of clothing. That way you can take things off and put them back on depending on the changing weather or your changing activity level.

Page 21: Which fabric would be best would depend on the season and weather during which each sport took place.

Index